THE
SUNSET
OF
STEAM

The Swartberg dominates GMA/M No. 4072 as it
heads 'The Cape Midlander' between
Snyberg and Barandas (21 April 1987)

A TRIBUTE IN COLOUR TO THE GOLDEN YEARS OF STEAM LOCOMOTIVES IN SOUTH AFRICA

THE
SUNSET
OF
STEAM

DENNIS MOORE

CHRIS VAN RENSBURG PUBLICATIONS (PTY) LIMITED PO BOX 29159 MELVILLE 2109 JOHANNESBURG

To my wife Jenny,
without whose patience, help,
encouragement and understanding
none of this would have proved possible; and
to my son Calvin,
whose date of introduction into service
(14 April 1988)
enabled him to share in some of
steam's final years.
I hope he remembers them!

Published by

CHRIS VAN RENSBURG PUBLICATIONS (PTY) LIMITED

Cor 11th Avenue and Main Road Melville P O Box 29159 Melville 2109
Telephone: (011) 726-4350/1/2 Johannesburg Republic of South Africa

The Standard Edition – English ISBN 0 86846 062 1
The de Luxe Edition – English ISBN 0 86846 064 8

First Edition Copyright © August 1990

Design: Michael Barnett MCSD
Photo-Lithographers: McManus Bros (Pty) Limited, Johannesburg
Printers: The Penrose Press, Johannesburg

All the photographs in this book are the work of Dennis Moore and
are being published for the first time.

Contents

Acknowledgements

No photographer can readily set out to produce a work such as this without the assistance of a great many people, railwaymen and enthusiasts alike. I would therefore like to thank those who have helped in various ways over the years.

First, South African Railways officials who readily produced the paperwork to enable visits to be made to their various premises. In many instances, as one becomes known to local railwaymen and management, these forms tend not even to be asked for, such is the friendliness and co-operation I and many others have received. Particular thanks to many at the Kimberley Regional Office, notably Dennis Beech, Hannes Loubser, Wicus Pretorius and – on the operating side – James Gordon and Chris de Lange. At Beaconsfield loco depot the footplate staff, depot foremen and supervisors went out of their way to assist.

A big thank you to one and all, particularly to Harry van Wyk, Jan van Aardt, 'JJ' Hanekom, Pat Abbot and Peter Odell. Thanks also to drivers at other depots: Don Pretorius and Willie Jansen (Krugersdorp), Messrs Kleynhans, Deysel and Jonck (De Aar), and Messrs Pretorius, Van Rensburg and Barnardo (George). To those others who readily gave assistance – anonymously – I offer equal thanks.

Numerous enthusiasts gave freely of their knowledge and assistance over the years. I am thus indebted to Tony Attwell, Bryan Benn, Nathan Berelowitz, Douglas Capewell, Christine Durrant, Dusty Durrant, Tony Gerrard, Steve Hardy, Allen Jorgensen, Charles Lewis, John Middleton, Ian Pretorius, Jenny Pretorius, Peter Rogers, John Strathern and Geoff Turner. Special thanks to my regular companions when chasing steam over the past few years: Martin Ward, Jean Dulez, Simon Leppard and last, but not least, my wife Jenny. Ultimately however, the greatest thanks must go to my parents, Anne and Syd Moore, for not discouraging me in my formative years from an interest which, to this day, they still do not quite understand.

Upon seeking publication of this work the immediate enthusiasm of the publisher, Chris van Rensburg was immense and was sustained throughout the project. My thanks both to him and all the staff at Chris van Rensburg Publications (Pty) Ltd and to the designer Michael Barnett.

Introduction

One o'clock in the morning. The alarm bell rings. After a fully rejuvenating night's sleep of ninety minutes one finds it difficult to summon up the energy to even venture outside on a freezing Transvaal morning, let alone face up to what lies ahead: a six hundred kilometre drive to Orange River, hopefully to locate a steam hauled train somewhere around sunrise. The rest of the day will be spent ricochetting up and down the line in an attempt to record a worthwhile image on three and a half centimetres of film. Overnight, at a lineside hotel, what sleep that is on offer will be frequently interrupted by the passage of trains (tolerable if they are steam but how irritating to be woken by the nauseating whine of a diesel). Alternatively, the night may be spent photographing at a servicing stop, frozen fingers trying to manipulate flashgun, camera and tripod, the brain so numb from exhaustion that it fails to warn your feet of signal wires or other obstructions into which one stumbles frequently. A further day of frenzied activity – or, even worse, hours waiting for activity which never materialises – followed by another marathon drive home. And for what? Why do we do it? I hope that the answer lies within these pages, expressed in the universal language of the photograph.

Since mid 1982 I have been documenting the final years of the steam locomotive in South Africa. I have no special interest in early railway history or the highly technical side of railways or locomotives, my interest is that of the observer of these mighty machines in action. I have been privileged to undertake many footplate trips but, from choice, these are relatively infrequent. The experience only serves to heighten my admiration for the men who – day in, day out – conquer these noble beasts of steel, fire and water. There is no doubt that, in creating the steam engine, man produced a living machine that could display beauty, elegance, power and yet instantly command awe. How many other machines have brought tears to the eyes and a lump to the throat of grown men, both observers and those involved in their daily operation? A steam locomotive is part of a team, with the driver and fireman fellow team members. At the end of a long, hard shift (often more than twelve hours in South Africa) the crew will feel they have – through their teamwork – accomplished something positive. Somehow, that feeling is not likely to be present with the crew of a diesel or electric locomotive. On the line, the steam engine is rarely a total casualty, usually being able to clear a section so as to avoid delay to other traffic. Not so with other motive power – once it's ill, it's dead. Equally true is the old driver's saying that with a steam loco it takes five minutes to find a fault and twenty-four hours to put it right, with a diesel it takes twenty-four hours to find the fault and five minutes to fix it.

I have no intention of covering historical matters or intricate technicalities; far more able pens than mine have covered such aspects. This book is intended simply as a memento for the thousands who find pleasure in the steam locomotive. The coverage is that of the sunset years – the final decade. With the planned phasing out of steam from everyday commercial operation during 1992 such coverage, perforce, commences during 1982. Many facets of steam operation are shown during this period: the humble shunter, the last passenger trains, the heavy freights, special tours, steam at night, steam in industry. No attempt has been made, however, for the coverage to be all-embracing. It would have been a relatively simple matter to include all lines that saw steam working during the period in question, but to what purpose? It would be pointless to include, say, a photograph of a grubby 19D at work on the scenically deprived Theunissen-Winburg line at the expense of a more scenic photograph of a 24 on the Knysna line. Similarly, no attempt has been made to include photographs of every locomotive class that has steamed since 1982. It is conceded that particular emphasis has been placed in this work on the 25NC and 26 classes. The former has been rather meagrely served in earlier publications which have mostly depicted as wide a spread of locomotive types as possible. As the backbone of South African main line steam power in the eighties, such space distribution is justifiable. In the case of the sole class 26, is apology or explanation necessary? It is certainly my favourite locomotive and judging by the attention it receives in the overseas railway press, I am not alone in such a preference.

I received much well-meant advice before leaving Britain (apart from the expected harbingers of doom on the socio-political scene). The railway view was that "It is too late . . . there is so little left to see . . . only expected to last a couple of years . . .". The fact is that, since mid 1982, it has been possible to photograph more than seventy classes in steam working in South Africa. That is a conservative total as it does, for example, harbour all the variations of North British built 4-8-2 tanks in one 'class'. For the record, from personal observation, the table on the following page lists most of the locomotive types concerned.

These have been observed on the S.A.R. network, in industry and in the hands of preservationists – the latter an activity that is still at an early stage in this country. What is more surprising is that representatives of at least 45 of these types could still be seen in steam during 1989.

It is, then, not surprising that South Africa has remained, throughout the 1980s one of the principal attractions for steam enthusiasts around the world. True, countries like India and China offer far more action, but with them come difficulties of climate, accommodation, transport, language, food and many other adverse factors. It is pertinent to record that South African Transport Services, recognising the attractions of its steam fleet, issued a press release during 1989 assuring its many foreign visitors and local enthusiasts that a degree of mainline steam working would remain until 1992 and that, thereafter, a designated route would be operated as a steam line on a permanent basis. In addition, many 'prestige' locomotives would be retained around the country to facilitate the operation of special passenger trains. South African Railways are to be congratulated on this response, which represents a far more enlightened approach than has been seen in most other countries around the world. The recent major overhaul of several museum locomotives for active service is particularly noteworthy, as was the 'Great South African Steam Train Festival' organised by the Cape Northern Region of South African Railways during September 1989. Nonetheless, it remains a matter of fact that, at the time of writing (June 1990), there remain only some 200 steam locomotives in everyday commercial service with South African Railways. Compare that with the approximately 1 000 that were in active service eight years earlier. Again, at the time of writing, the following services remain steam worked on a regular basis:

Kimberley-De Aar (main line)
George-Knysna (branch line)
Virginia-Glen Harmony (branch line)
Loerie-Patensie (narrow gauge)
Port Elizabeth-Loerie (narrow gauge – not daily).
Various shunt and trip workings, some of which are quite lengthy, operated by locomotives based at Germiston, Springs, Kroonstad, Kimberley and (occasionally) Pretoria, Krugersdorp, Humewood Road depots.

One secondary line survived into 1990 with steam traction, that from Kimberley-Bloemfontein, but from March diesels took over the remaining steam workings. Additionally many depots around the country maintain locomotives for special workings, some of which are very frequent (e.g. Johannesburg-Magaliesburg trains worked by Krugersdorp based locomotives, Johannesburg-Heidelberg by Germiston locos, 'Trans Karoo' express worked most Fridays by a Braamfontein based Class 25NC).

Functional steam locomotives for occasional operation may be found at depots with no everyday steam activity, such as Witbank, Bloemfontein, Queenstown, Sydenham, Voorbaai, Wentworth, Bethlehem, Waterval Boven and, probably at some time in the near future, Cape Town.

In addition to S.A.R. activity, there are still other steam worked railways of interest. No less than 25 industrial sites remain wholly or partially steam worked. Also, of major importance is the privatised Alfred County Railway now operating the narrow gauge line between Port Shepstone and Harding. On the subject of narrow gauge one should remember that, by international standards, all the locomotives depicted in this book are narrow gauge. Yet such is the sheer size and power of many South African steam locos that there is really no adjustment for the eye to make. Who, for example, would look at the 191 tons of a GMA/M at Randfontein Estates Gold Mine and describe it as an industrial narrow gauge tank engine – which technically it is?

Finally, I must acknowledge that – in the sunset years – many of the more scenic routes have long since switched over to retrograde traction. However, it is hoped that this book achieves its aims – to present a balanced selection of scenes from the glorious golden sunset years of steam in South Africa. With luck the final sunset will end in perpetual twilight.

D. MOORE
Roodepoort, South Africa

June, 1990

A	7A	14CRB	16DA	25	NG/G11		North British 2-6-2 T
B	7C	14R	16E	25NC	NG/G13		North British 4-8-2 T
C	8B	15A	19A	26	NG15		North British 4-8-4 T
1	8C	15AR	19AR	S	NG/G16		North British 4-8-2 T/T*
1A	8DW	15BR	19B	S1	NG/G16A		North British 4-8-0*
1B	10CR	15CA	19BR	S2	Manning Wardle 0-4-0 T	North British 4-8-2
3BR	11	15CB	19C	GEA	Bagnall 0-4-2 T		Other Builders 0-4-0 ST
4 AR	12A	15E	19D	GF	N.Z.A.S.M. 0-4-0 T		Other Builders 0-6-0 ST
6	12AR	15F	23	GL	0-4-0 fireless		Other Builders 2-6-0 ST
6A	12R	16CR	24	GMA/M	0-6-0 fireless		Other Builders 0-8-0 T
				GO	0-8-0 fireless		Other Builders 0-6-2 T
							Other Builders 2-6-2 T
							Other Builders 4-8-2 T

(* rebuild)

Free State Finale

1

Few would deny that the Bethlehem–Bloemfontein line was amongst the most scenic in the days of steam. Loads were not heavy but the topography of the area guaranteed exciting railway action. The two towns are little more than 200 km apart as the crow flies, but the railway is forced to take an often twisting 300 km route, the eastern half of which was particularly attractive from the photographer's viewpoint. □ Bethlehem was home to most locomotives that worked this line, although Bloemfontein supplied some motive power, particularly for shorter distance workings on the western section. Bethlehem town was founded in 1864 on a river that early settlers named the Jordaan (after the biblical Jordan), long ago dammed to form Loch Athlone. Initially the line passes through a prosperous agricultural region, but soon the railway is flanked by the Witteberge on the northern side, a constant companion for the next 100 km or so. The principal geological features of the area are many huge outcrops of striated sandstone rock, one of the more prominent of which is called Soutkop, situated at Sekonyela, and few indeed must be the railway photographers who have been in the vicinity and not photographed a train passing this well known landmark. □ 100 km from Bethlehem lies the town of Ficksburg, in the centre of an area noted for its extensive cherry orchards. It was founded in 1867, at the close of the Basuto war, on the banks of the Caledon River, which forms the boundary between the Free State and Lesotho. Shortly after leaving Ficksburg the line crosses a tributary of the Caledon on a girder bridge in an attractive setting and here the international border is only 3 km from the railway, the Maluti Mountains in Lesotho (often snow-capped in Winter) forming a

Opposite: The Witteberge is an imposing backdrop to 25NC No. 3402 at the head of the eastbound passenger train, seen here just prior to its brief stop at Meynell halt (11 May 1985).
Above: 25NC No. 3409 blasts off from Barnea with the overnight Bloemfontein-Bethlehem passenger train (11 May 1985)

backdrop to the southerly view from the line. □ 170 km out from Bethlehem is Modderpoort, a turning point for shorter distance workings from either end of the line, and also the junction for a short branch line to Ladybrand. Anxious in their quest to follow the trains, few enthusiasts probably realised that in rock shelters in the steep hill behind the railway station could be found fine examples of prehistoric rock art, as well as a cave church that is still in use. Once the railway emerges from the poort the scenery is generally duller, although one or two pleasant spots could be found, particularly in the Thaba 'Nchu district – the principal settlement in an isolated section of Bophuthatswana. Before that, at Marseilles, a 26 km branch line heads south east to Maseru, the capital of Lesotho and that country's only rail trackage. □ Eventually, after a near 10 hour journey, the passenger trains would arrive at Bloemfontein and it was a ride to be remembered. Sadly, it is no more. The passenger trains were dieselised during 1986 but, perhaps not co-incidentally, this led to their total demise a year or two later. The loss of steam on passenger trains threatened to pose a problem for weekend visits to the line as, at that time, it was only they that ran on a Sunday. However, with a stroke of genius, the Operating Department then regularly scheduled two or three freight trains to depart from Bethlehem on a Sunday afternoon. □ Sadly, this was to be a short lived utopia – the general diesel infestation commenced during 1987 and by October of that year it was all over, or so it seemed. Recently, 25NC No. 3410 was restored to service at Bloemfontein and stationed at Bethlehem for special duties and, just prior to Easter 1990, the line once again played host to the sight and sound of steam action at its best.

Opposite: Rich tones of umber create a warm scene as
25NC Class pioneer No. 3401 pulls away from the Brandlaagte passing loop
with a westbound Sunday freight (5 July 1987)

Above left: 25NC No. 3421 heads the westbound passenger around an S-bend
between Ficksburg and Owanty. The Maluti Mountains in the background are
in Lesotho, the international border being only three kilometres distant
at this point (14 June 1986)

Above: The eastbound passenger with No. 3402 laying a smokescreen over
the landscape between Owanty and Ficksburg (11 May 1985)

Left: Another Sunday afternoon freight leaving Brandlaagte
(between Slabberts and Sheridan) behind No. 3419.
The rebuilt ex-condenser tenders are not particularly attractive,
but matters are helped when the paintwork is clean

Opposite: The eastbound passenger train, seen here behind No. 3411 crossing a tributary of the Caledon River just west of Ficksburg, the principal intermediate town on the eastern section (14 July 1986).
Above: The section of the route between Sheridan and Slabberts was renowned for its many photogenic spots.
At about 5.00 p.m. (12 October 1986) 25NC No. 3419 heads for Bethlehem with the daily passenger train, seen here near Sterkfontein

Above: The daytime eastbound passenger seen *(left)* behind No. 3401 on 26 May 1985 at Sterkfontein and
(right) with No. 3419 in charge pulling away from Generaalsnek on 12 October 1986.
Below: 25NC No. 3420 climbs out of Slabberts with a westbound freight (5 July 1987)

25NC No. 3401 at the head of the eastbound passenger,
seen here at the well-known photographic location a km or so
before Meynell halt (26 May 1985)

Sun, Sea, Lakes and Forest 2

It is indeed fortunate that the last steam worked Cape gauge branch line of substantial length in South Africa, and the last home of the Class 24 2-8-4s, is the highly scenic 67 km line that runs from George to Knysna in a popular holiday area. Diesels made an appearance on the line a few years ago, but did not stay for long. At present the branch remains the domain of eight Class 24s, allocated to Voorbaai depot where they receive repairs and washouts, but at any one time five are sub-shedded to George. Daily requirements call for a mixed train each way Monday-Friday, together with one or two return goods trains. Additionally, a pilot loco is required at George for shunting, often two to cover early and late shifts. The daily mixed conveys two carriages at the rear and is popular all the year round with both tourists and locals alike. During peak holiday times, when the train runs on Saturdays as well, additional passenger coaches are added and the train then often runs solely as a passenger service. The locomotives are maintained in immaculate condition, in standard black and highly decorated, with one each in blue and green livery. In addition, a GO 4-8-2 + 2-8-4 was recently transferred to the area for occasional use on the line. □ With two or three trains operating daily, the line offers tremendous scope for photographers, albeit that the weather is extremely changeable in these parts. Eventually though, one should force oneself away from the lineside and spend a day riding the mixed, the journey taking a little over three hours each way and guaranteeing a memorable experience. □ Leaving George, the first part of the run is downhill through forestry areas along the Meul River Valley and it is this section, on the return trip, that provides a real challenge to the locomotive's abilities. There are glimpses of the sea at Ballots Bay, but close contact with the coast is first made at Victoria Bay, the little halt being perched immediately above the beach – a popular surfing spot. A short tunnel follows

Opposite: Class 24 2-8-4 No. 3684 storms through the woods at Keytersnek halt (22 June 1989). *Above:* The morning freight from Knysna to George, seen just west of Goukamma behind Class 24 No. 3660 (27 June 1989)

and then the train swings out onto a bridge across the mouth of the Kaaimans River, probably the most photographed railway location in the country. From the train there are superb views both up the river and out to sea. There is a further tunnel and then come magnificent views of the 8 km long Wilderness beach, before descending into Wilderness station where the train usually stops to allow the schedule to catch up. Under way again, the train gradually moves inland, as it crosses the Touws River three times, the last on a combined road/ rail bridge. The train now enters the Lake District, with Lower Langvlei, Upper Langvlei and Rondevlei being passed in succession on the south side. It then runs alongside the largest lake, Swartvlei, before crossing it on a low bridge and continuing into Sedgefield station. Here is the likeliest place for the train to be crossed by the returning early morning goods, and – without fail – the Sedgefield Post Office tricycle will be there to collect the mail that has travelled down from George. □ After Sedgefield, the train follows the full length of Groenvlei, the only freshwater lake in the district, before heading into another extensive afforested section as it winds down into the Goukamma Valley. A heavy climb is encountered as the train enters a horseshoe curve, then a succession of twists and turns before Keytersnek is reached. Staying in the forest Belvedere is passed as the delightful vista of Knysna lagoon comes into view. The lagoon dominates the view on the left hand side of the train until Brenton. Here the line turns to run straight across the lagoon on a long low bridge until the picturesque town of Knysna is reached. After an hour or two the train sets off back to George, the return offering many different and pleasant views. □ For how long this delightful state of affairs will remain is a matter of conjecture, but if the wishes of many of the local residents were to be heeded, it would be indefinitely.

Above: The author has lost count of the number of times he has struggled to reach this vantage point on the west bank of the Kaaimans River at its mouth with the Indian Ocean. Following a lengthy walk and an arduous climb through thick bush the photographer's usual reward, even if the weather is otherwise fine, is for a breeze to blow in off the ocean forcing the smoke down alongside the locomotive and train, thus ruining the shot. After several dozen attempts, all the elements co-operated on 26 June 1989 – patience has its rewards. Class 24 No. 3683 does the honours with the returning mixed train. *Opposite:* No. 3693 climbs out of Goukamma with the Knysna mixed (17 August 1983)

Moods of the Swartvlei: The Swartvlei, west of Sedgefield, is the largest of the lakes in the district and offers varied photographic opportunities, whatever the time of day or the vagaries of the weather.
On the opposite page *(above)* 24 Class No. 3693 heads the Knysna bound mixed (17 August 1983), whilst No. 3622 is seen *(lower left)* on the return working of that duty on the previous day.
No. 3660 is seen *(lower right)* late on the morning of 27 June 1989, returning to George with a freight, whilst *(above)* the tranquil waters of the vlei reflect the progress of No. 3683 at the head of the outward mixed on the following day

Shortly after Goukamma station, Knysna bound trains face a severe climb as the line twists and turns for several kilometres
before reaching Keytersnek. No. 3683 struggles with the mixed just prior to hitting the horseshoe bend.
In thirty seconds the 2-8-4 will be heading in completely the opposite direction, only to swing around again shortly thereafter (28 June 1989)

Look through any railway book and 'going away' shots are noticeable by their absence or scarcity.
The opportunities should not be ignored, however, as clearly demonstrated by No. 3617 and No. 3653 heading an eastbound
passenger train near Duiwerivier shortly after dawn (10 April 1985)

The photographic opportunities for trains returning from Knysna
at least equal those of the outward run. No. 3684 is seen *(above)* with the mixed,
between Brenton and Belvedere (22 June 1989).
The Knysna Lagoon is visible in the background

Four days later, sister locomotive No. 3683 was on the same duty and
is seen *(above right)* storming up to Bleshoender halt.
Many overseas visitors have taken photographs near this little halt
but, probably, few realised quite how strange the name is when translated –
'Bald Chicken'! At noon on the next day, No. 3660 is seen crossing
the Kaaimans River Bridge near Wilderness with the returning freight *(right)*

Above: The dark blue liveried
No. 3632 during a lull in pilot activities
at George (28 June 1989)

When 15F No. 3108 was outshopped from Bloemfontein works on 15 September 1988,
it was feared that this would be the last steam locomotive to receive a major overhaul.
Since that time, however, policy has changed and several locomotives
have received heavy overhauls. The majority have been for special duties,
but amongst them were two Class 24s for everyday service on the George-Knysna line.
These were ex-works during 1989 and, even more surprisingly,
came out in non-standard liveries, No. 3660 in an attractive shade of green,
with a sister engine in dark blue. The green locomotive is seen *(above)* on the return of
the morning freight, high above Victoria Bay on 22 June 1989 and
(right) four days later climbing towards Belvedere on the same duty

The Rearguard

3

If, as is now expected, regular commercial line operation by steam on South African Railways ceases during 1992, then the rearguard action during the final decade commencing mid-1982 will have been fought over 40 separate lines, six of them narrow gauge. The retreat has been quite steady. By the latter half of 1982 there were four losses, of particular significance were the scenic Maclear-Sterkstroom line and the intensive suburban service at Port Elizabeth. Burgersdorp-Rosmead was, perhaps, the saddest of the seven losses in 1983, but in 1984 there was a slow down in the carnage, with just one casualty. The years 1985/1986 saw a reduction of ten, the most significant feature being the decimation of most of the remaining narrow gauge trackage. The rearguard fought on valiantly, but a further four were lost in 1987, most significantly the Bethlehem-Bloemfontein line. 1988 saw a further eight go, mostly in the Eastern Cape, but also two in the north of that province. This left six – as discussed in the introduction to this book – to be reduced to five with the dieselisation of the Kimberley-Bloemfontein line as from March 1990. □ Surprisingly, during 1989 there were no further losses – the Rorke's Drift of South African steam, perhaps? This has been particularly strange given the withdrawal of older diesel and electric power

that has been taking place. By 'older', of course, one refers to diesels and electrics with barely 30 years (and, in many cases, significantly less) service. Meanwhile, some steam locos with well in excess of 60 years service soldier on in everyday use – long may they do so. □ It should be emphasised that in many cases the change in motive power was followed by the demise of the line concerned: Queenstown-Tarkastad, Molteno-Jamestown, Fort Beaufort-Seymour, amongst others. (One can draw one's own conclusion). In other cases, the lines were closed outright but on those that remain, it is rather curious how many trains that were formerly handled without a problem by a solitary steam locomotive, now require two of the 'modern' motive power units. □ It is not my intention to discuss the merits of various types of traction, nor is there a need to do so. S.A.R. itself conducted an investigation into the economics of steam, diesel and electric power allied to extant traffic levels on the Kimberley-De Aar line. As is now well known, steam came out ahead of the pack, but it seems the policy decision had already been made. □ This chapter is primarily a pot-pourri of scenes that were current during some of the sunset years but now – except for special occasions – have succumbed to the march of 'progress'.

Many of the final duties of steam in South Africa are on shunt and trip workings and Germiston shed, just a few kilometres to the east of Johannesburg, still retains 15CA and 15F locomotives for such workings. Sadly, however, the sturdy S1 0-8-0 shunters were not to survive until the very end. One of their last turns was to shunt the wagon works adjacent to the shed and (above) No. 3814 is seen so engaged on the evening of 7 December 1983. When this last S1 duty was withdrawn, their replacements were 15CA locomotives, twenty to thirty years their seniors. Two S1s are pictured (opposite) enjoying their Sunday rest at Germiston shed (29 August 1982)

Many of the branch lines that survived into the sunset era with steam power were worked by 19D 4-8-2s, which were supplied in several batches between 1937 and 1948. Bethlehem housed several of the type, one of which was outstationed at Warden for working the daily mixed train to the junction with the main line at Harrismith. No. 3361 is seen *(left)* near Balmoral with the return working on 7 April 1984, passenger accommodation being rather more copious than usual on this occasion. From time to time, the branch locomotive made an additional run to Harrismith in the late afternoon on a goods train, and No. 3361 is again seen at Balmoral *(lower left)* on such a working (18 May 1985). Grahamstown, with its lines to Alicedale and Port Alfred, was another centre for the 19Ds, and No. 2759 is seen *(below)* backing out of Grahamstown shed yard on 23 July 1982, prior to commencing its day's work

The 278 km long branch from Sterkstroom to Maclear in the Eastern Cape was also the domain of the 19D 4-8-2s, but steam working survived long enough to fall within the timescale covered by this book, the line being fully dieselised at the end of the winter season in 1982. No. 2770 and No. 2741 are shown *(above left)* about to stall near Haselton shortly after sunrise on 5 August 1982. Soon thereafter, the lead engine was declared a failure and it was abandoned, along with half the load. No. 2741 carried on and is seen *(left)* climbing out of the horseshoe curve at Birds River

Evoking memories of past days, the first special steam working on the line after dieselisation crosses the Tsomo River near Cala Road *(above)* behind No. 3351 and No. 2746 (4 April 1983)

Above: A matching pair of semaphore signals enhance this shot of Class 24 No. 3687 leaving the electrified main line at Nylstroom and setting out on the 74 km branch to Vaalwater (15 October 1983). The line was fully dieselised on 23 September 1985. *Opposite:* Another branch worked by the lightweight Class 24 2-8-4s was that from Cookhouse to Somerset East, which fell victim to the diesel during April 1988. During the final winter season, No. 3667 heads the return mixed train away from Somerset East across the Little Fish River Bridge, the scene dominated by the Bosberg

The last daily passenger trains on South African main lines to be regularly steam powered were those on the
Mafikeng-Vryburg-Warrenton route. A 25NC sets out from Mafikeng at 6.40 a.m. on 9 September 1984, with a 4 1/2 hour
run ahead of her. At Vryburg, a sister engine will take over for the remainder of the run to Warrenton

Another 25NC on the southbound passenger a few km south of Mafikeng (22 November 1987).
A storm the previous day had left considerable surface water lying in the vicinity.
This was to be the last summer of steam on the line, diesels taking over during the following May

Early in 1987 a dispute arose between Botswana and Bophuthatswana, which prevented Botswana Railway diesel locomotives from crossing the international border to reach Mafikeng. To break the impasse, trains were worked between Mafikeng and Rakhuna (a crossing place 11 km into Botswana) by South African Railways. What made this specially interesting was that steam was used, thus once more offering the photographer the chance to photograph main line international steam hauled trains. For over a year – until diesels took over the duty – Mafikeng shed provided two well maintained 25NC locos for these trains. 25NC No. 3519 heads a northbound just south of the international border, a social weavers' nest being prominent in the picture (September 1987)

A latter-day haunt of the veteran 15AR 4-8-2s was the Port Elizabeth area, where the class remained active on shunt and trip working until late 1988. Their most famed exploits, however, were on the Uitenhage run, the last intensive steam hauled suburban train service in the world. Fifty minutes for 32 km may not appear too demanding but with nine intermediate stops, some lightning acceleration and hard running was called for from these engines with their relatively small 57 inch driving wheels. Perhaps the most visited photographic location on the line was between Swartkops and Redhouse, where it was occasionally possible to obtain clear reflection shots in the waters of the mud flats.
In addition to the suburban passengers, the odd freight turn had to be fitted in as well. *(Left)* No. 2018 heads towards Uitenhage with a freight where, a few minutes earlier, No. 1969 had rushed past with its trainload of commuters bound for their offices in Port Elizabeth *(right)*. The date was 19 July 1982 and dieselisation of the service was only two months away. It is perhaps not surprising that, when diesels took over, the frequency of the service was reduced by half, S.A.R. probably realising that, thenceforth, many people would prefer to drive to work

Above: The Balfour North-Redan line remained steam worked until August 1987 with a daily return pick-up duty, typified by 15F 4-8-2 No. 3003 seen *(left)* crossing the Bosrivier Bridge on the outward run (22 December 1984). Occasionally, a somewhat more substantial train would venture onto the metals, such as 12AR No. 1535 heading an eastbound special passenger *(right)* across the same bridge (23 July 1983)

Right: The amazing sight, on 3 September 1988, of a steam hauled commercial freight on the Steelpoort branch which had been dieselised since May 1972. The local populace could hardly believe their eyes and many cars were parked on the road bridge to the potential detriment of the photograph. Just to oblige, however, the two veteran 15CA locomotives, No. 2850 and No. 2056, took off southbound from Santa in an explosion of smoke and steam that wiped out the opposition and created a magnificent sight notwithstanding the appalling weather

The attractive little station of Magaliesburg saw its last daily steam train in June 1984. But, here, more than anywhere else in South Africa, steam was to fight back with a vengeance. By the latter half of the eighties, steam passenger trains were arriving here from both Pretoria and Johannesburg with an average frequency in excess of once a week. Additionally, trains occasionally venture out further west, to Syferbult and beyond. Magaliesburg itself also sometimes sees locomotives arriving on test freight trains from Krugersdorp where many prestige locomotives are housed and maintained.

Two of the more unusual happenings are shown here: *(Above)* Class 6A 4-6-0 No. 454 (owned by the Railway Preservation Group) demolishing a vehicle in a spectacular fireball at Doringspruit, some 12 km out of Magaliesburg (7 February 1987). *(Right)* An early departure from Magaliesburg saw 15F No. 3153 greeting the dawn 10 km to the west near Watershed, bound for Mafikeng (13 April 1987)

Newly restored GF 4-6-2 + 2-6-4 No. 2401
heads a westbound passenger train through
Tarlton station (4 March 1990)

Driver Don Pretorius leans out from the cab of 19D No. 3323
as his train nears Magaliesburg, from the Pretoria direction,
under gathering clouds heralding a summer storm (3 December 1988)

Nocturne

4

Few who have witnessed the sight would disagree that a steam locomotive acquires a special magic at night. On the move, its headlight pierces far into the dark, while the air is filled with a crescendo of power and action, especially in the stillness of winter. As the locomotive hurtles past, the observer catches a brief glimpse of exhaust, thrashing motion, the burning heart of the firebox, the crew hard at work. Then, suddenly, it is all over, save for the fading sound of the train climbing on, on, into the night. □ On shed, the magnificent machines take on an even more menacing aura. More so, at an intermediate servicing stop, where the fires are cleaned, the burning, golden coals tumbling down between the tracks. Thirsty tenders are replenished and fires built up, the safety valves lift, a huge white plume rushes into the freezing air to join the stars. Receiving the road, they set off once more into the endless depths of darkness, grappling with their load. Who can say they are not moved by such a scene? Such is nocturne . . .

Opposite: At 1 a.m. Bethlehem's shed pilot, 19D No. 2720, rests on a damp and eerie night amongst the willow trees near the coal stage (29 May 1982)

Left: The same locomotive is seen still resident in its personal nook, nearly ten months later (25 March 1983)

Above: One of the last surviving Class 14R locos, No. 1707, works a Sunday night shunting turn at Krugersdorp station (23 May 1982)

Right: Narrow gauge 4-6-2 tank NG4 No. 16 lurks in a quiet corner of De Aar shed yard during July 1982, seemingly forgotten. Its working days with S.A.R. ended in Natal during 1948 but the engine then put in more than 20 years service with its new owners (Rustenburg Platinum Mines) before being returned for preservation. After many years storage, the locomotive now resides at the Humewood Road narrow gauge museum in Port Elizabeth

Opposite: The last survivor of the S2 class of lightweight 0-8-0 shunters was No. 3706, here seen at Waterval Boven shed during the early hours of 7 June 1982. Outliving her sisters by several years, No. 3706 was retained for shed pilot work, which duty she performed for the last time on 1 March 1985, when Waterval Boven closed to steam

Opposite: A pair of 19Ds and a 12AR while away the night hours at Beaconsfield shed, Kimberley (8 August 1982)

The sole Class 26, the world famous 'Red Devil' looks particularly impressive at night due to its striking livery. Two views of the locomotive are shown above whilst it is being serviced at Orange River, the mid-way point on the Kimberley-De Aar main line. *(Above left)* Shows fire cleaning in progress during the early hours of 23 January 1989, whilst *(above right)* the fresh paintwork positively glistens during the evening of 16 September that year. *(Below left)* A somewhat grubbier No. 3450 prepares to depart from her home shed at Beaconsfield, Kimberley (5 May 1989)

Above: Shortly before midnight three Class 25NC 4-8-4s stand in repose at Bethlehem shed (4 March 1983).
Opposite: The unusual sight of immaculate 15CA No. 2828 heading 25NC No. 3514 at Orange River
during the evening of 20 September 1989 on a De Aar bound freight

Double headed 25NCs (No. 3484 and No. 3516)
being serviced at De Brug, at the head of a
Kimberley-Bloemfontein freight (21 January 1989)

Another view of No. 3484 and No. 3516 at De Brug
a few minutes before the resumption of their journey
to Bloemfontein, just 50 km distant

One o'clock in the morning of 29 August 1988 and
it is freezing at Orange River as the 'Red Devil' prepares to
do battle with the long climb that lies ahead

Well worth missing a night's sleep for! Water cascades down No. 3450's tender as servicing
proceeds on this southbound double headed combination, the second locomotive being the last serviceable
condensing Class 25 No. 3511 (Orange River, 16 September 1989)

Twin Steel

5

The 235 km long double track main line from Kimberley to De Aar has established it-self as one of the principal railway attractions in the world. Although scenically unexciting, the sheer experience of main line action draws enthusiasts from far and wide. This part of the Karoo is not as flat as it seems – the gradients are quite significant and they are often prolonged, calling for sustained hard work. The sight of double headed 25NCs forging south from Orange River with 40 loads of coal in tow is not one that is easily forgotten. It will be a sad day, indeed, when the twin steel no longer resounds to the power of steam.

Opposite: The pride of De Aar shed, 25NC No. 3481, in her usual immaculate condition, heads south from Beaconsfield yard with a freight destined for her home town (22 July 1989). *Right:* A pair of 25NC 4-8-4s forge south out of Orange River, the first weak rays of the morning sun highlighting their billowing exhausts (18 June 1989)

Above and opposite: The Beaconsfield South shunter is greeted by the
first rays of a glorious sunrise, as she busies herself making up trains which her
more fortunate sisters will later head south to De Aar (12 June 1988)

A pair of 25NCs
charge south through Poupan on 18 June 1989
under a brooding winter sky

This locality gives the finest grandstand view on the entire 235 km route, yet is seemingly one of the least known and rarely visited by photographers. From this point, northbound trains can be observed crossing the Orange River Bridge, turning through 90 degrees, and then climbing steadily for a couple of kilometres – a magnificent scene for film makers. Here, 25NC No. 3516 is seen on a lengthy freight at 6 a.m. on the 25 November 1987

Opposite: (Above left) Two of De Aar's 25NCs, No. 3481 and No. 3431, hustle a southbound coal train through Graspan (23 September 1989). *(Lower left)* 25NC No. 3481
climbs Enslin bank on a southbound freight during the afternoon of the 22nd July 1989. *(Above right)* 25NC No. 3431 heads a southbound night train at
Orange River (16 September 1989). *(Lower right)* Driver Jan van Aardt is in charge of No. 3536 seen rushing through Kraankuil station on a De Aar freight (Autumn 1989).
Above: A few kilometres north of Heuningneskloof station, 16E Pacific No. 858 races along with a southbound freight (27 June1988). A few seconds after this photograph was taken,
the front section of the left side coupling rod snapped in two, causing a rapid and ignominious halt. Repairs were effected a few weeks later by a transplant from sister engine No. 857,
preserved on her plinth outside Bloemfontein station. The donor was soon to see better days herself, entering Bloemfontein Loco Depot for repair.
Missing parts were specially manufactured and No. 857 received a nine year boiler certificate during March 1990 and is expected to return to 'prestige' train service later in 1990

'Smoke please' – not a problem as 25NC No. 3529 departs in an eruption from Belmont station on 6 May 1989 with
the southbound Saturday 'mixed' (a freight which conveyed a coach at the rear for passengers).
Belmont station was used by the British during the Boer War as a hospital and casualty clearing point during the advance on Kimberley

No. 3432 and No. 3501, heading a
train of hopper wagons, tackle the northbound climb
out of Modder River (22 September 1989)

The Narrower Narrow Gauge

Most railway lines in South Africa were constructed to the narrow (by international standards) 'Cape Gauge', that is 3′6″ or – strictly converted – 1 067 mm. (Incidentally, the gauge is now officially referred to as 1 065 mm. One wonders what happened to the missing 2 mm). A few lines, however, were built to the still narrower gauge of two feet. Those that survived into the 1980s comprised four separate systems in Natal – which were totally decimated by outright closure between 1983 and 1986 – plus the 283 km line from Port Elizabeth to Avontuur with a branch to Patensie. □ Today, the only narrow gauge to survive under S.A.R. auspices is the line in the Cape Province and that is largely diesel worked. Steam still survives on the Patensie branch, however, and a freight on the eastern end of the main line is steam hauled occasionally, to change over locos for the branch. In addition, the narrow gauge

Opposite: The coal trimmer appears to be enjoying the ride as NG/G13 2-6-2 + 2-6-2 Garratt No. 60 bids welcome to the rising sun at Edinglassie with the thrice weekly train from Umlaas Road to Mid Illovo. This quaint line was the last home to this class of 'baby' Garratts and, sadly, closed completely during March 1985. First introduced in 1927 the design was most successful and culminated in the NG/G16 class (which differed only in minor details), examples of which were built as recently as 1968. *(Above)* Before dawn on 17 April 1987 NG/G16 No. 131 stands in Port Elizabeth docks prior to departure on a charter passenger train

beach area. □ In Natal, three of the four systems were wantonly cast aside. However, the fourth, that from Port Shepstone to Harding was closed by S.A.R. in November 1986 but subsequently re-opened by a private company: the first common carrier railway line to be privatised in South Africa. The author is proud to be a shareholder in this enterprise. Now known as The Alfred County Railway, the trains are running once more – behind steam. Hordes of passengers are now carried on the 'Banana Express', although this covers only a portion of the route. The lifeblood of the line is freight: block trainloads of the area's main product (timber, not bananas!) are hauled the entire length of the line. Some of the trains load to more than 500 tons, not bad for a two foot gauge railway. As in the last years of S.A.R. operation NG/G16 Class locos form the motive power, although NG15 2-8-2s may follow in due course. Additionally, the

trackage in Port Elizabeth harbour returned to steam shunting in 1989 after many years of diesel operation. The 'Apple Express' still steams on, carrying tourists from Port Elizabeth to Loerie on certain Saturdays, and on other days by arrangement. In addition, a short haul passenger train was also recently introduced, with steam power, to a popular Port Elizabeth

Railway has recently introduced into service the prototype NG/G16A locomotive – essentially a 'mini-Red Devil'. □ This section of the book illustrates several facets of S.A.R. operation on the narrower narrow gauge in the sunset years. Hopefully, what now remains will be with us for some time to come.

Right above: The inhabitants of the Zulu village have more sense than to venture outside at sunrise on a cold winter's day. Only the photographer witnesses the passage of NG/G16 No. 140 as it nears Donnybrook on a dual gauge section of track with a freight from Ixopo (26 June 1984)

Right below: The Alfred County Railway's prototype NG/G16A No. 141, decked out in its 'Red Devil' livery,
drifts into Izotsha with the morning freight (28 February 1990).
The little locomotive is popularly known as 'The Red Dragon'

Opposite: NG15 2-8-2 No. 124, a regular performer on the 'Apple Express', is on less familiar territory as it threads through the Gamtoos River Valley with a special passenger train destined for Patensie (8 April 1985).
The Gamtoos, believed to have been named after a Khoikhoi tribe living in the area, is notorious for its unpredictable flash floods

Another view *(above)* of NG15 No. 124 on 8 April 1985, this time on the
return journey on the climb out of Hankey. The NG15s are surprisingly
powerful engines for their size and gauge. On a tractive effort basis they
compare with most variants of the Cape gauge 6th classes or, as a further
example and making allowance for the differing basis of calculation, with the
British Railways Standard 2MT 78000 series 2-6-0. The two scenes *(right)* were
taken on the Port Shepstone-Harding line, which was abandoned by S.A.R.
during November 1986, but subsequently re-opened as the privatised
Alfred County Railway, commercial operators of both passenger and freight
trains. The upper view shows NG/G16 No. 156 on 29 June 1984, during S.A.R.
days, returning to Port Shepstone amidst scenery typical of the line; whilst
maroon No. 116 is *(lower right)* heading the morning freight on the rejuvenated
A.C.R., seen here climbing out of the horseshoe curve between Shelly Beach
and Izotsha on 1 March 1990

The Kouga Mountains form a backdrop to
NG/G16 No. 131 racing the shadows on a returning
Patensie-Gamtoos charter train (17 April 1987)

Above: The same train, as depicted on the previous page, here seen crossing the Gamtoos river just south of Hankey.
Opposite: The strikingly red liveried NG15 No. 122 piloting NG/G16 No. 131 near St Albans on the first stage
of a special passenger working from Port Elizabeth (17 April 1987)

Winter's Breath

7

The majority of overseas visitors who come to South Africa to witness steam's golden years do so during the months of May, June, July and August when the air is crisp and cold and the sky a clear, cobalt blue. Such conditions are ideal for photography, particularly for early morning effects, with the white exhaust hanging motionless in the air. Such effects occasionally obtained as early as April or as late as October. In some ways, winter visitors miss out as the quality of light late on a summer's afternoon when a rainstorm has cleared the sky, takes some beating. Still, there is no decrying winter's attractions.

Opposite: No. 3413 climbs up to Retiefsnek with a Bethlehem bound freight. It was a very cold day as evidenced by the steam effects, even though the photograph was taken at 11.00 a.m. (4 July 1987).
Right: The floods of the previous summer left a legacy of several substantial expanses of water adjacent to the Kimberley-De Aar line, put to good use here as 25NCs No. 3432 and No. 3523 head a heavy coal train a few kilometres north of Kraankuil (24 July 1988)

Right: 25NC No. 3409 gets to grips with a Modderpoort bound freight on the initial climb out of Bethlehem (28 July 1982)

Below right: During March 1983 25NC No. 3416 hurries east of Fouriesburg with the overnight Bloemfontein-Bethlehem passenger. Quite possibly this is the last photograph ever taken of this particular locomotive at work as – a few days later – it was one of a pair of engines wrecked in a tragic head-on collision at Barnea

Below left: Lingering traces of winter hang in the air as No. 3481 and No. 3437 double head a northbound freight near Spytfontein (October 1988)

25NC No. 3501 is a magnificent sight
as she heads a De Aar bound freight out of Beaconsfield Yard
shortly after sunrise (22 September 1989)

Left above: 19D 4-8-2 No. 2723 leaves Ugie with the Maclear-Sterkstroom passenger train (2 August 1982)

Left below: Into the '90s. Modified 25NC No. 3454 climbs up towards Potfontein with a De Aar freight (23 June 1990)

Above: The 'Red Devil' heads south near Potfontein on a freezing morning (22 June 1990)

Opposite: A pair of veteran 15AR 4-8-2s (No. 2100 and No. 1784) storm out of Bethulie on the final lap of their run to Springfontein with a special train (7 April 1983)

Above left and right: 16E 4-6-2 No. 858 working a lengthy morning freight from Bloemfontein to Kimberley, is seen *(left)* approaching Kloofeind and *(right)* departing from De Brug (6 May 1989)

Left: No. 3440 and No. 3486 with a freight for Bloemfontein, on the climb up to Olienhoutplaat (26 July 1986)

Opposite: 25NC No. 3413 leaves a steam and smoke trail to mark its passage east of Ficksburg (4 July 1987)

Inter Provincial

8

The last secondary main line in the country to remain steam worked was that from Kimberley, Cape Province to Bloemfontein, Orange Free State. It was not an exciting line scenically, but offered tremendous scope in the use of lighting. Being orientated on an east-west axis there was much potential for sunrise and sunset photographs. The working timetable saw many changes in schedules on this line over the past few years and the degree of steam working varied from day to day. The train which offered the greatest likelihood of successful photography became almost legendary: the 3.15 p.m. fast freight from Kimberley to Bloemfontein. Regularly scheduled to be double headed, by the late 1980s this working undoubtedly attained the status of the most photographed freight train in the world. Although overall speeds on the 160 km line were sometimes slow, due to single line working and the need for frequent crossings with opposing trains, once on the move the trains frequently set a fast pace. Whilst lacking the glamour of a double track main line, many enthusiasts had a far higher regard for the Kimberley-Bloemfontein route than the adjoining Kimberley-De Aar one. It would have been an ideal candidate in many ways, for the 'permanent steam line' referred to in the introduction but, seemingly, this possibility has already been ruled out, the route losing its final regular steam duties in March 1990.

Opposite: 25NC No. 3508 was in fine condition, climbing well at Driekloof with an eastbound freight (11 July 1987).
Above: Two locomotives, four chimneys . . . and making the best use of them to upset the environmentalists. Modified 25NC No. 3454 leads the black 'Red Devil' in an assault upon the Kloofeind bank (6 September 1986)

28 June 1988: The beginning.
Well before dawn, 25NC No. 3449 heads west through
Perdeberg with a freight for Kimberley

28 June 1988: The end.
Just before sunset No. 3476 and No. 3444 hustle
the '3.15' through Immigrant

15F 4-8-2 No. 2928 shunts the silos at De Brug,
having worked in on a pick-up freight
from Bloemfontein (18 June 1988)

25NC No. 3484 nears the summit of
the five mile 1 in 70 climb from Olienhoutplaat
at Kloofeind station (11 July 1987)

Opposite: (Above) Condenser No. 3511 doubleheads the modified 25NC No. 3454 on the renowned '3.15', seen here 3 km west of Perdeberg (21 January 1989).
(Lower left) No. 3450 and No. 3454 hurry through Immigrant with an eastbound freight (19 June 1988). *(Lower right)* An eastbound 25NC hauled freight is looped at Immigrant (6 May 1989).
Above: The Modder River looks peaceful enough as a 25NC hauled freight drifts nonchalantly across the bridge east of Perdeberg (6 June 1987).
During the following summer, however, there was devastating flooding in much of South Africa, causing widespread death and destruction.
Both the Kimberley-Bloemfontein and Kimberley-De Aar routes were closed to traffic for a time, but some lines around the country were completely washed away in parts.
At this particular river bridge, the waters were lapping the base of the girders at the height of the floods.
Nonetheless, this fared much better than the lower lying road bridge nearby, which at one point was submerged under twenty-five feet of water

Running with its 'parking lights' on, the modified 25NC No. 3454
leads the Condenser No. 3511 on the '3.15', a few kilometres before
the first service stop at Perdeberg (23 July 1988)

The same combination as shown on the previous page,
but this time with the Condenser in the lead, as the pair race
through Petrusburg station (21 January 1989)

Wheels of Industry

9

As the 1980s drew to a close, there remained 25 or so industrial sites where steam locomotives were still in regular use – most, but not all, utilising redundant S.A.R. power. Coal, gold and platinum mines, power stations, sugar and paper mills, and a water pumping station; the range of users was matched only by the diversity of liveries that the locomotives wore. Coal mines tended to feature the more spectacular operations and hence have received fair coverage in other publications. To redress the balance it is appropriate to look now at some of the gold mining activities together with one or two other aspects of industrial railway activity. ☐ Certainly the most spectacular industrial steam operation today is the 28 km route of the Randfontein Estate Gold Mining Company situated on the West Rand, linking three operating shafts with three reduction plants and laid out in such a manner that complete diversification of operation is possible. During 1982 R.E.G.M. presented a dismal sight to the enthusiast: two diesel locos on ore haulage and one ex-S.A.R. steam loco in use daily pottering around on stores or shunting duties. Just the sort of unexciting picture described by Messrs Lewis and Jorgensen in 'The Great Steam Trek' when they lamented the decline of the railway and commented how very sad it was for those who had seen this short-lived operation in its prime. I am sure those two authors are as pleased as anyone that they have been proved wrong. By 1983 two new shafts had been opened, served by a brand new railway laid to main line standards. They were followed a few years later by a third located at the end of a new 8 km long branch line. The motive power: massive GMA/M Garratts, painted in an attractive blue livery lined out in yellow. The livery was not to last long, changing within a year or two to a stunning maroon lined in black and gold. Ex-S.A.R. locos of classes 1, 14R and 15BR worked alongside the Garratts initially until the number of the latter in service had increased sufficiently. ☐ This expanded operation had a somewhat shaky start, more than one serious head-on collision caused several locomotives to be written off. A further incident in

Opposite: Under an unsettled sky, No. R16 (4059), in a grubby maroon livery, clambers up to Cooke Reduction Plant (10 October 1984). *Above:* A sight for sore eyes at the R.E.G.M. Cooke Plant servicing point as several GMA/M locos are prepared for their next shift (10 May 1986)

April 1985 led to the rapid installation of a full CTC signalling system and since then the network has operated satisfactorily. The spate of accidents led to a shortage of serviceable locos, only 3 GMA/M plus the Class 1 being available in mid-1985. (The diesels, underpowered and very slow, had been withdrawn by February 1984). Consequently, several 15F 4-8-2s were hired from S.A.R. and operated for most of the remainder of that year, albeit on reduced loads. ☐ By the close of 1985 matters began to settle into the magnificent operation that can be seen today. The locomotives are once again in a blue livery (almost Caledonian blue) but with gold and black lining. There are currently 12 on the roster, all GMA/M save for a solitary 15BR reinstated to service in the late 1980s. Current requirements call for six locomotives to be in daily service; they are worked very hard indeed, twenty four hours a day, six days a week. There is little doubt that these locomotives work far harder now than they ever did in their S.A.R. days. The sight and sound of one of these Garratts storming up the steep climb to Cooke plant with a 1 000 ton block load of ore, minutes after sunrise on a summer morning is worth travelling a long way to see. (The fact that the author has chosen to live just 20 minutes drive away from such action is not a coincidence!) ☐ Another prime attraction during the sunset of South African steam was, and remains, the Welkom area gold mines. Largely dieselised in the 1970s, a change of policy resulted in the magnificent sight of, for example, 86-year old 2-8-2s hard at work in 1990. Unlike the coal mines, the area displays a great diversity of attractive liveries, and the locomotives enjoy a high standard of maintenance and cleanliness. ☐ Some enthusiasts have tended to ignore industrial steam operations, but in South Africa this is a serious omission. Large locomotives, often working very hard, are worth more than a passing glance. They play an important part in keeping the wheels of industry turning and are likely to continue to do so for some years. Hopefully, the turn of the century may yet see a few steam stalwarts soldiering on.

Opposite: On Sunday 10 July 1983 a special passenger train was run over the Randfontein Estates Gold Mine system, ostensibly to mark the opening of the new line to Cooke 3 shaft but, doubtless, also to celebrate the introduction into service of the GMA/M class of 4-8-2 + 2-8-4 Garratts – surely the most impressive motive power fleet of any industrial operation in the world. On this occasion the coaching stock was loaned by the Railway Society Preservation Group, providing a fine venue for the directors of R.E.G.M. and its holding Company J.C.I., together with their guests. Flags of both R.E.G.M. and J.C.I. were carried by No. R10 (ex-S.A.R. 4084), seen here in the afternoon approaching the Millsite Uranium Plant. R.E.G.M. has been magnificent in its support of the Preservation Group, which was pleased to be able to offer a little something in return on this day.

Above: (Left) It is not yet 5.30 a.m. on 1 January 1990 and a finer way to see in a new decade is hard to imagine. A GMA/M storms up to Cooke Reduction Plant with a standard 1000 ton block trainload of gold ore.

(Right) Christmas Eve 1988: There is a minute break in an otherwise totally overcast dawn as a GMA/M struggles up the final kilometre of the long climb to Cooke Reduction Plant

Towering storm clouds gather menacingly over GMA/M No. R11 (4123) as she runs with a block load of ore between
Cooke 2 and Cooke 1 plants at the southern end of the R.E.G.M. system. Within seconds of these photographs being taken, the author was caught
in one of the most violent thunderstorms he has experienced and visibility rapidly became non-existent (11 January 1986)

15BR 4-8-2 No. R7 (ex-S.A.R. 1990) scurries along with a wagon of stores near the Millsite Uranium Plant (4 November 1988).
At the time of writing No. R7 is the only 'straight' locomotive to remain operable on the R.E.G.M. roster and
still puts in a good day's work on stores and shunting duties notwithstanding her 70 years of service

15BR No. R3 (1982) heads a train of manganese powder about 1 km into its journey from
the Millsite Uranium Plant to the main Cooke complex.
The train has just passed under the main Krugersdorp to Potchefstroom S.A.R. line (26 January 1985)

Opposite: (Above) A portrait of No. R16 (4059), ex-works in the summer of '86/'87, during a service break at Cooke 3 shaft, the southern extremity of the R.E.G.M. system.

(Lower left) A GMA/M heads a load of ore destined for the reduction plant at Doornkop, past the junction of the lines to Cooke 2 and Cooke 3 shafts (11 January 1990).

(Lower right) No. R12 takes the main line just north of Midload junction, the Doornkop branch just discernible in the background (December 1985).

Above: No. R11 (4123) on the lengthy haul from Cooke 3 shaft to Millsite reduction plant, a return run of more than 40 km with a ruling gradient predominantly against loaded trains calling for sustained hard work. The train is seen emerging from a wooded area onto a substantial embankment located between Cooke plant and SD32 shaft (2 August 1986)

One of the attractions of industrial locations besides the diversity of locomotive types to be found, is the variety of colourful liveries employed. Freegold is the largest gold mining company in the world, processing more than 20 million tons of ore a year. The northern region of Freegold retains an extensive steam worked rail network comprising the trackage of the former Western Holdings and Free State Geduld systems. Their locomotives were painted in attractive liveries, maroon and green respectively; when Freegold was formed in 1985, a common (revised) livery was sought. A most unattractive plain dark blue was tried out but was fortunately short-lived; a two tone grey livery with a gold band was then applied to some locomotives. This was a pleasant colour scheme, but evidently did not wear well. One or two engines were then repainted in the former F.S.G. green but, eventually, by the close of the 1980s, a decision to standardise on the former W.H. maroon was made. The upshot of all this was that a visit to the complex in 1988 could produce seven different locomotive types in four different liveries. To demonstrate the wisdom of the eventual decision, two views, taken on 24 May 1986 of locomotives in the W.H. maroon livery are shown on these pages. *(Above)* 4-8-2 No. 7 (S.A.R. 3BR 1482) heads a train from No. 6 shaft to the reduction plant, whilst *(opposite)* Class 11 2-8-2 No. 6 (923) is seen en route to No. 7 shaft. Both these photographs were taken in the vicinity of the triangular junction roughly equidistant from the three producing shafts. Of particular note is the age of these veterans – at the time of writing 78 and 86 years old respectively and still in everyday service

The green and the two-tone grey liveries referred to earlier are shown above. *(Above left)* A Free State Geduld system 4-8-2, 19BR No. 8 (ex-S.A.R. 1410) hauls a load of ore on 16 March 1985 from Freddies shaft, the northernmost point of the complex. Since the formation of Freegold, ore is sometimes railed from one system to the other, depending on operational requirements. This results in the connecting line, previously used only for occasional stores movements, seeing fairly frequent traffic. This was obviously not anticipated when the Welkom golf course was laid out, as a more formidable golf hazard is difficult to envisage! *(Above right)* No. 1, a standard North British built 4-8-2 tank, churns up the fairway (21 May 1988).

(Lower left) Perhaps the most elegant of all the locomotives remaining in everyday industrial service. No. 771, a 10CR Pacific dating from 1910, is in exemplary condition as she poses for her portrait on 14 April 1985 – a credit to her owners, Loraine Gold Mines Limited, one of several mines in the Welkom district which has remained loyal to steam

Away from the mining sector, there are many other owners of steam locomotives engaged in various facets of industry. More typical of British industrial locomotive practice, the saddle tank has always been a rarity in South Africa. One of the few examples of this type is 'Elizabeth', an 0-6-0 st kept in immaculate condition at Orlando Power Station in Soweto and seen *(above left)* during a break from shunting (13 May 1989). Rail traffic at the Rosherville workshops of ESCOM dwindled rapidly during the 1980s and, by 1985, their locomotives were rarely used, although all were cosseted. They were steamed from time to time. *(Above right)* A line up of an 0-4-0 st, a 2-4-0 tank of Jersey Railway origin, the famous 'Kitty' a 4-6-0 tank now 111 years old and declared a National Monument – and, in steam, 'Hunslet', a 2-6-0 st which is a comparative youngster at 88 (14 July 1985). By early 1990 'Kitty' remained with ESCOM for special duties, her sisters having been loaned to various worthy bodies for preservation. One of the less frequently photographed industrial locomotives is 'Komati', an 0-6-2 tank belonging to Dunns Locomotive and Boiler Works of Witbank, seen *(left)* working a train down to the exchange sidings situated alongside the S.A.R. locomotive depot (23 August 1985)

Above left: Loraine Gold Mines played host to a special passenger train on 14 April 1985. 10CR 4-6-2 No. 771 and 19B 4-8-2 No. 1407 make a superb sight as they pass the junction to No. 2 shaft along an immaculately maintained permanent way

Above right: Even the setting sun fails to bring much colour to a troubled sky as No. 771 returns a load of empties to Loraine's No. 3 shaft (18 June 1983)

Right: One of Rustenburg Platinum Mine's own 15CB Class 4-8-2s works a train of ore near the Bleskop Reduction Plant (6 July 1985). In recent years, most workings here have been handled by 15CA locomotives on hire from S.A.R. but the system is now rumoured to be a candidate for early electrification

A stunning black, green and gold livery was a feature of
the President Steyn Gold Mine Class 11 2-8-2s of which No. 6 'Stella Steyn' (ex-S.A.R. 929)
is seen at work on 23 July 1988, a mere 84 years of service behind her!

The Devil Rides

10

Locomotive No. 3450, a standard 25NC, entered Cape Town's Salt River Works during November 1980. When it emerged just over three months later a metamorphosis had taken place and the glistening red machine, now designated Class 26, became the celebrity locomotive of South Africa's final decade of steam. The time in the workshop was, of course, merely the final phase. Design work on the conversion had commenced in September 1979 and was finalised in mid-1980. Several months then elapsed whilst component parts were manufactured. Major modifications comprised the incorporation of a gas producer combustion system, double Lempor exhaust, an extended smokebox, an enlarged superheater, new piston valves and valve gear improvements, revised main steam pipes and steamchests, improved mechanical lubricator, air sanding and a host of other detail improvements, not all of which subsequently survived the rigours of everyday service. The striking livery adopted – an unusual shade of red – commanded attention from the outset. Christened 'L.D. Porta' – later 'Soekie' – the locomotive is rarely referred to as such. At birth, the Salt River workshop staff dubbed No. 3450 'Die Rooi Duiwel' ('The Red Devil'), a name which has stuck ever since, even during periods when the locomotive was painted blue or black! □ Over the years the locomotive's external appearance changed with the original Czechoslovakian type smoke deflectors giving way to large round topped deflectors, the fall plate being removed for some time and then re-appearing, the feedwater heater being removed and other minor mechanical modifications being made. The original livery gave way to a dark blue, which did not suit the loco at all. This was soon replaced by standard black, which suited it even less. Later, the deflectors were repainted red and slowly but surely various parts below running board level came to be picked out in red. In this guise the 'Devil' looked reasonably impressive but during July 1988 common sense and the popular vote prevailed and the loco was returned to its original all-over red livery, without, however, the tender being lined out. □ On the performance side, the exploits of the locomotive have been legendary, both during its periods on test at Pretoria – largely working the Witbank line – and in everyday service based at Kimberley. Impressive coal and water savings and increased power output were proven beyond doubt. Granted, the 'Devil' can be a little slippery but it was not designed as a shunter or to haul pick-up goods trains. On an express passenger or fast freight, the 'Devil' has astounded many and is without equal on the 3′6″. The loco lost a little of its bite as certain modifications were dispensed with, partly at the behest of the maintenance staff who are sometimes not too enthusiastic about non-standard design features. By any rational assessment, No. 3450 should have formed the basis of a complete refurbishment programme for the 25NCs, but it was not to be. Seemingly regardless of the results achieved, the negative decision had already been made. □ On a brighter note, the locomotive was outshopped on 11 April 1990 after an intermediate overhaul at Beaconsfield depot. The 'Devil' rides on!

Opposite: 'The Red Devil' pilots the sole operable Class 25 through Petrusburg station on a Kimberley-Bloemfontein freight (29 October 1988). *Above:* Czechoslovakian-type smoke deflectors were particularly fitting for the Class 26 as first rebuilt and from an aesthetic viewpoint it is unfortunate they were not retained. No. 3450 hurtles past the south signal cabin at Beaconsfield with the southbound 'Orange Express' on 13 July 1982, just the sort of duty to which the locomotive is suited

On 11 June 1983 'The Red Devil' was used to work
a passenger train from Pretoria to Witbank,
its final day's work in the Transvaal following a period
on test. Looking superb in a new coat of paint
(indeed some of it was still wet!),
No. 3450 is seen *(above right)* backing off
Capital Park shed and later
(below right) departing from Bronkhorstspruit,
about halfway on the outward run

Opposite: 'The Red Devil' at night.
Waiting for the road out of Orange River,
No. 3450's regular driver 'JJ' Hanekom attends to
the fire whilst his fireman surveys the scene
from inside the cab, which is as immaculate as
the outside of the locomotive (16 September 1989)

The weather had been awful all afternoon on 23 February 1985 but for a couple of minutes the sun shone brightly from a tiny chink in an incredibly dark
stormy sky illuminating a small portion of the track at Witput. Just at that moment, a northbound freight deigned to arrive
but no ordinary loco was at its head . . . rather 'The Red Devil' itself, checked momentarily by adverse signals, safety valves lifting . . .

. . . A few seconds later No. 3450 received the road and pulled away past the famous lineside hotel at Witput,
safety valves still screaming and under a veil of smoke. Before half the train had passed the photographer the sun had vanished,
not to re-appear for the remainder of the day. Sometimes everything just comes right!

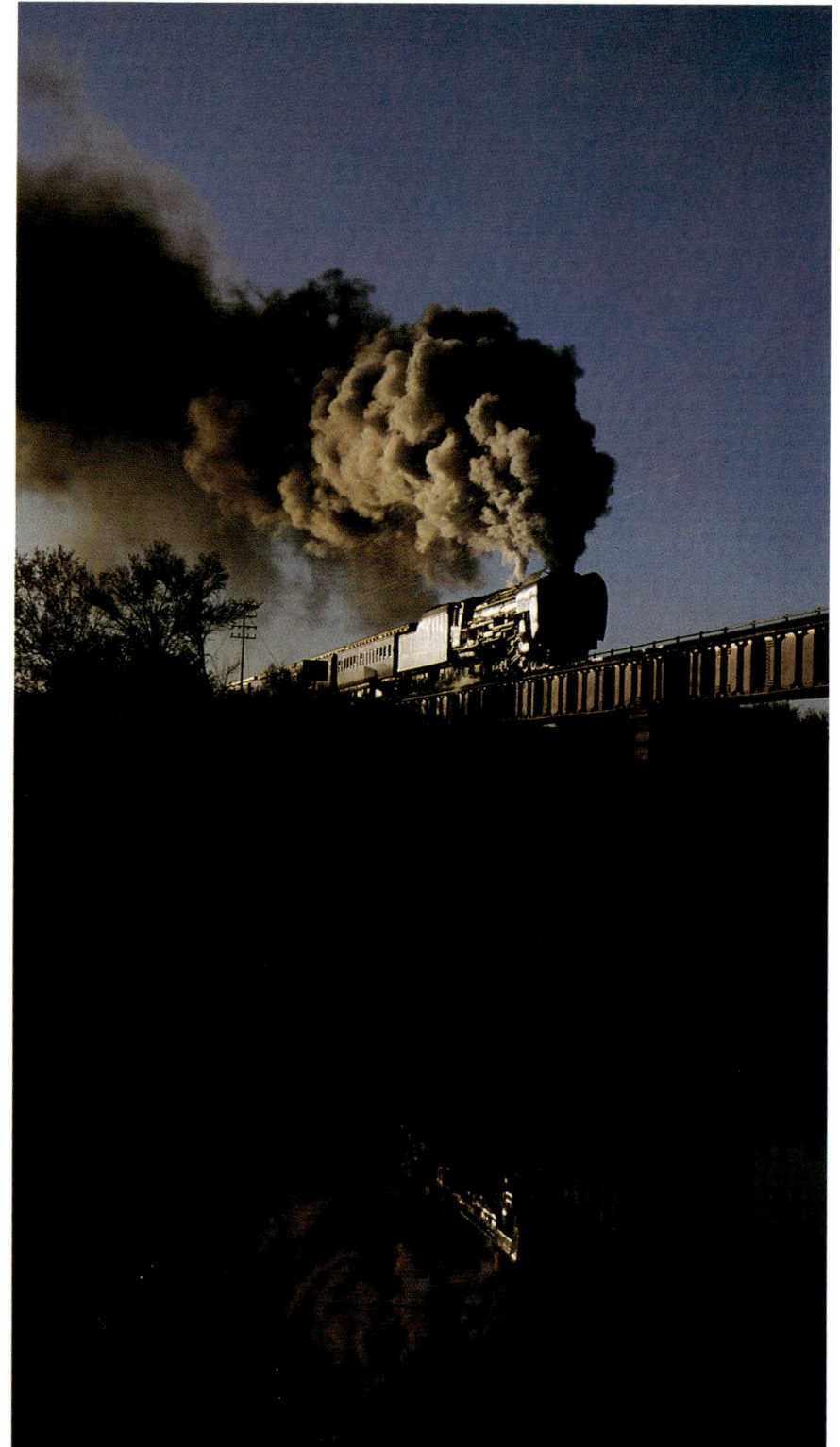

Towards the end of 1985 someone decided to repaint 'The Red Devil' in
a dark blue livery. It was awful but, by careful choice of lighting, one could
continue to photograph the locomotive to some effect.
Three such scenes are shown here, all taken during the early morning
of 31 March 1986 at the Modder River Bridge at Perdeberg on
the Bloemfontein-Kimberley line. *(Above)* No. 3450 gingerly crossing
the bridge well before dawn, its passengers beginning to stir
as some minutes later the train reversed back down to the bridge
to deposit them at the lineside. A few moments afterwards,
(right and opposite)
the 26 performed a stirring runpast for those
prepared to forsake their breakfast cornflakes

Right: Within a few months an even worse atrocity was inflicted upon No. 3450:
standard black livery relieved only by a white line along the running board.
Looking its worst, the locomotive is seen here on 6 September 1986 at the
Bloemfontein Showgrounds, with a Kimberley bound freight.
Fortunately some degree of common sense was soon to reassert itself and
this drab all-over black livery was destined to be shortlived

Below: Slowly red began to re-appear on the locomotive – first on the smoke deflectors,
then gradually on many other parts. By 1988, No. 3450 actually looked quite impressive
in its two-tone livery. On 18 June 1988 the 'Devil' was paired with No. 3454 on an
afternoon freight from Kimberley to Bloemfontein and they are seen in these
two photographs a few kilometres either side of Perdeberg

At around 6.00 a.m. on a beautifully clear summer morning, No. 3450 slogs up the grade near Behrshoek with a northbound freight.
This initial 20 km climb from De Aar is the only sustained hard work for Kimberley bound trains on the southern section.
From the summit down to Orange River the grades are generally favourable and No. 3450 was soon to take advantage of this with some very fast running (23 January 1989)

Steam Renaissance

11

The Railway Society of Southern Africa and/or its associated preservation groups and the Railway Museum frequently run special trains in various parts of the country. These vary in scope from short one-day tours to those lasting up to two weeks, the latter traversing some of the most scenic routes in South Africa, many of which have not seen regular steam working for several years. Thus, even in these final sunset years, the photographer has scope for recording steam at work in fine surroundings. Scenes from selected tours appear in this chapter, accompanied by a glimpse of one of several locally organised special trains which have run in recent years and are aimed more at the general public than the enthusiast market.

Opposite: The train is reduced to insignificance by the grandeur of the scenery through which it passes. 19D No. 2746 heads a special passenger train seen here at an early stage of its journey on the Aliwal North-Barkly East line, which is noted for its ruling gradient of 1 in 30 as well as the numerous reversing stations necessary to overcome the formidable obstacles of nature (6 April 1983)
Right: 'The Umgeni Limited' departs from Steelpoort, powered by GMA/M 4-8-2 + 2-8-4 No. 4122. The town is dominated by the foothills of the northern part of the Drakensberg range (6 April 1988)

The 157 km route from Graaff-Reinet to Rosmead, incorporating the Lootsberg pass, was one of steam's more revered haunts in the 1970s and the author was privileged to witness the last few days of regular activity during a visit to South Africa in 1979. Such photographs, of course, fall outside the ambit of this book but this is not so with the several special passenger trains that have subsequently worked the line. A pair of 24 class 2-8-4s, No. 3620 and No. 3667, joined forces on 3 April 1983 and are seen (*left*) powering 'The Mountaineer' near the summit on the northbound climb of the Lootsberg

Making a superb sight in a striking landscape, is 19D No. 2714, together with the last operable 12R No. 1505.
Their train is 'The Cape Venturer' and is pictured during the early (and easier) stage of the journey out of
Graaff-Reinet (7 April 1986)

Left: The section of line connecting George with
Oudtshoorn is only 74 km long but includes the majestic
Montagu Pass, another line that sadly lost its steam
power during 1979 but, as with the Lootsberg, has
subsequently seen several special trains including at
least one steam hauled freight in recent years.
Shown here are two views of one such special working –
'The Trans Cape Limited' which ran over the Pass
on 10 April 1985.
19D No. 2714 and GMA/M No. 4072 grapple with
the final stretch of the line to the summit at Topping

Right: GMA/M No. 4072 threads
'The Cape Midlander' through Stompdrift, prime
ostrich breeding country, whilst working the
Oudtshoorn-Klipplaat section (21 April 1987). The
previous year 'The Cape Venturer' broke new ground
by being the first steam train to enter Cape Town
station for many years. To get there involved much
travelling 'under the wires', which reduced
photographic possibilities. Making the best of it,
however, is 25NC No. 3481 seen *(lower left)* stretching
out near Draai on the final part of an overnight journey
to Touws River (1 April 1986). Two days later GMA/M
No. 4072 draws the train away from Ashton, somewhat
intimidated by the bulk of the Langeberg which
dominates the area *(lower right)*

Between Klipplaat and Oudtshoorn the Tarka River passes through a defile in an otherwise impenetrable natural barrier known as Toorwaterpoort ('Magic Water Gap'). When the railway builders arrived in the area they had little choice but to share this route and the result was one of the most memorable audible experiences available to a traveller on a steam hauled train. The sound of the locomotive ricochets off the sheer walls of the poort and has to be heard to be believed. Several steam hauled special trains made the eastward run through the poort in the Sunset Years of Steam, rather rarer is the westbound 'Trans Cape Limited' seen on 9 April 1985 behind 19D 4-8-2 No. 2714

Right: GMA/M No. 4072 drags 'The Cape Midlander' out of the shadows of the Swartberg (21 April 1987). A different viewpoint of the action in this most attractive location is shown as the frontispiece of this book

Below: Seeing double on the Barkly East line! 19D No. 2746 on 'The Mountaineer' contrives to be in two places at once at Reverses 7/8 on 6 April 1983

Below right: Class 24 No. 3682 teams up with GMA/M No. 4072 on 'The Cape Venturer' to skirt the hopfields near Camfer on the downhill run from the summit of the Montagu Pass (5 April 1986)

The Graskop branch line runs through extensive forestry areas in an attractive part of the Eastern Transvaal. Double headed Class 24s (No. 3688 and No. 3643) power 'The Selati Limited' on the return run from Graskop (22 April 1984) and are shown *(left)* in scenery typical of the line. Upon arrival back at Nelspruit these locomotives were replaced by GMA/M No. 4122 for the journey along the main line to Waterval Boven, the 24s being scheduled to follow the passenger train as they too had to return to the shed at Boven. At a point between Waterval Onder and Waterval Boven, arrangements were made to allow passengers to photograph the Garratt working the train. A clutch of photographers duly assembled on the vacant track and No. 4122 set back a good distance to commence its runpast. What was not immediately realised is that this section of the main line is signalled for bi-directional working and so, with 'The Selati Limited' having halted in section, the Class 24s were switched to the adjacent track and forged ahead regardless. Thus the photographers obtained the result shown *(opposite)*. Bearing in mind where they were standing, some may have thought it was to be their last picture!

Above: GMA/M No. 4122 nears Spekboom on the Steelpoort branch at the head of 'The Umgeni Limited' (6 April 1988).
Opposite: Sister locomotive No. 4072 brings 'The Cape Venturer' through beautiful scenery between Snyberg and Barandas on the Oudtshoorn–Klipplaat line (6 April 1986)

Other organisations besides enthusiasts' groups charter special steam hauled trains and the northern portion of the Steelpoort branch has been a popular venue. One such train ran from Lydenburg to Burgersfort and back on 2 November 1986 and three views of the train are shown on this page and opposite.
Right: GMA/M No. 4122 swings around by the main road near Mantsibi; the lower view is also roadside – this time at Rusplaas.
Opposite: The train is just south of Ohrigstad, the low sun bringing out the colours of the Jacaranda tree and the adjacent ramshackle hut

Steam Festival

12

During the middle of 1988 it seemed that the enthusiasts' world was about to end. Rumours circulated of imminent full dieselisation of the Kimberley-De Aar line, with the Bloemfontein line logically to follow soon thereafter. The resultant howls of anguish were followed by letters of pleading and protest from both within South Africa and abroad. Representations were made to S.A.R., the Tourism Board and politicians. □ Coincidentally or not, steam working was retained thereafter on both lines at reasonable levels. During 1989 a policy document on steam locomotives was published by South African Railways – as referred to in the introduction to this book. Furthermore, an amazing event was organised by the Northern Cape Region, primarily on the Kimberley-De Aar line, for the benefit of multitudes of visiting enthusiasts during the period 16-23 September 1989: The Great South African Steam Train Festival. Without doubt, an event like this on such a scale by a national railway administration was without precedent anywhere in the world. During the Festival, an intensive advertised programme of trains (freight, passenger and empty coaching stock) was worked by many prestige locomotives, including Kimberley's own 16E, 25, 26, modified 25NC; De Aar's 15CA No. 2828 – specially reinstated for the event; Class 23 and 15F, visiting from Kroonstad; and a

Opposite: Train No. 2431, the 10.00 a.m. from De Aar to Kimberley hammers through the sadly named Spytfontein ('Spring of Regret'). 15CA No. 2828 was past her sixtieth birthday but performed magnificently and it was a privilege to once more see and hear this famous locomotive type in action on the main line (18 September 1989).
Above: The 16E was a popular locomotive throughout the Steam Festival. No. 858 heads the 8.00 a.m. Kimberley-De Aar freight past the stone crushing plant just north of Spytfontein (22 September 1989)

GMA/M and Class 12AR which made the long trek from the Transvaal. All the locomotives mentioned were immaculate, those based at De Aar and Kimberley having been fully repainted for the event, as had several other 25NCs housed at the two depots. In addition to the advertised programme, many regular 25NC hauled trains were run. To ensure that high levels of steam working were maintained, regardless of the commercial traffic available, empty rakes of open wagons, hopper wagons and coaching stock were run when necessary. Driving and firing tuition was offered on the Douglas Branch and the 'Orange Express' was steam hauled in both directions throughout Bloemfontein-Kimberley-De Aar. The action continued day and night, with some trains timed to heighten photographic opportunities in early morning light. □ It was unfortunate that the event was not scheduled for mid-winter, a time more suitable for photography and that overseas advertising did not begin sooner. The relatively short notice given to foreign enthusiasts inevitably reduced their attendance, though that still turned out to be highly encouraging. Those present, enthusiasts and railwaymen alike, experienced a most rewarding time. All those in the Northern Cape Region who were involved in this excellent piece of organisation can look back on the occasion with pride.

One of the surprises of the Steam Festival was
to see De Aar's veteran 15CA No. 2828
running on the main line. This locomotive
was one of several that had seen only menial
shunting duties at De Aar during the 1980s
and by 1987 all had been laid aside as surplus
to requirements. However, after a couple of
years gathering rust, the locomotive was
repaired, repainted and performed superbly
on several days, her usual duty being the
10.00 a.m. De Aar–Kimberley freight with a
return late in the afternoon. Hopefully, the
authorities will retain No. 2828 for occassional
duties during the final year or two of steam
on the Kimberley–De Aar route. No. 2828 is
seen here heading her freight northbound at
Heuningneskloof station
(18 September 1989)

Replacing the usual two large diesels, 25NC No. 3481 handles the
17 coaches of the northbound 'Orange Express' with ease,
seen here crossing the Orange River and running well to time (19 September 1989)

The action continued day and night, to the extent that sleep became something of a luxury for the more dedicated enthusiasts. It was worth the effort, though, as memories of the night trains will long remain. Modified 25NC No. 3454 is seen *(above left)* emerging from the inky blackness at Witput station on 22 September 1989 heading a northbound freight, still proudly carrying the 'Orange Express' headboard – which train she had worked south earlier that day. 15CA No. 2828 *(above right)* takes water at Orange River in the company of 25NC No. 3431, with which it was working a De Aar bound freight during the night of 16 September 1989. During the early hours of 21 September 1989 green liveried 15F No. 2928 accompanied 'The Red Devil' on a nocturnal visit to Orange River en route to De Aar with an overnight freight *(below right)*. Incidentally, one had to feel sorry for the ash pit staff here who, having been used to coping with no more than 14 steam trains per twenty four hours, suddenly found themselves working frantically day and night with train after train powered by steam, many of them double headed

Opposite: No. 2828, No. 3450 and No. 3511 feature in a busy scene at Orange River on 16 September 1989, a third steam hauled southbound freight having departed a few moments earlier

On most days, a freight was booked to leave Kimberley at 6.00 a.m. – shortly before sunrise at that time of year. Fortunately, the train usually departed late enabling photographs to be taken soon after sunrise on the initial climb out of Beaconsfield Yard. Such is the scene on this page with the quite amazing combination of 23 Class 4-8-2 No. 3300 double heading GMA/M No. 4122 on a De Aar freight about 1 km south of the signal box controlling the exit from Beaconsfield Yard (19 September 1989). Who would have thought such scenes of a revenue earning freight train would be possible during 1989?

The same train is seen with conditions more like those expected in mid-winter, a bright sun
highlighting billowing white exhaust against a cobalt blue sky. The location is the southern end
of the distinctive row of poplar trees near Klokfontein

The colours clash somewhat as green 15F No. 2928 and red 26 No. 3450 climb up to Behrshoek *(left)* on 21 September 1989 soon after leaving De Aar on a northbound freight. Unfortunately, a gusting westerly wind was making photography rather difficult and by the time it had subsided it was close to noon with the sun very high in the sky. Nonetheless, on the opposite page, the pair make a pleasant sight steaming through Heuningneskloof station, one of many on the line that maintain well tended gardens even though regular passenger trains no longer call. High wheeled No. 858 steps smartly through Kraankuil station in the company of Class 23 No. 3300 *(below)* on a southbound goods during the previous afternoon. The 6'0" driving wheels of the 16E Pacific are the largest of any sub-standard gauge locomotive in the world

Above: Modified 25NC No. 3454 in full stride with the southbound 'Orange Express' near Klokfontein
(22 September 1989)

Below left: 16E No. 858 re-starts her De Aar bound freight out of Modder River station (22 September 1989)

Opposite: The S.A.R. went to much trouble to bring down the only operable 12AR 4-8-2, No. 1535, from her
Germiston home to the Northern Cape Region to participate in the activities. Unfortunately, the seventy year old
lady had a somewhat traumatic time of it, running hot on more than one occasion, rather disrupting laid down plans.
After many years of relatively tranquil duties, usually as Germiston station pilot, the prospect of 470 km return trips
on the Kimberley-De Aar route was perhaps a little daunting. Nonetheless, she made it a couple of times and is seen
here laying down a smoke screen in the company of 16E No. 858, whilst hauling a block load of cement south through
Heuningneskloof (18 September 1989)

Sunset of Steam

13

A chapter which needs no introductory comment concludes this work: 'The Sunset of Steam' – at sunset.

Opposite: A pair of 4-8-4s pull away from the water stop at De Brug during Spring 1989, with a freight for Bloemfontein, as the setting sun bids them farewell.
Right: The last rays of the setting sun illuminate the way ahead for the Class 26 on an eastbound freight at Driekloof

Class 26 No. 3450 and 25 No. 3511
make a memorable sight as they climb up through Driekloof
in the soft evening light (22 October 1988)

A GMA/M charges up the grade to Cooke plant on the R.E.G.M. system, with a heavy load of
gold ore, set against a magnificent twilight. Patience was rewarded – the sun had vanished below rail height at
least thirty minutes before this photograph was taken (19 December 1987)

Above right: Recently introduced into R.E.G.M. service,
GMA/M No. R6 catches the setting sun as she gets to grips with her load
away from Cooke 2 shaft; a long run to the Millsite reduction
plant lies ahead by which time it will have long become night
(3 June 1989)

Below right: A 25NC climbs the final kilometre into Modderpoort
with a freight from Bloemfontein (July 1982)

Opposite: The sun has just settled below the horizon as the last
working 25 Class Condenser No. 3511 and the sole modified 25NC
No. 3454 blast their way upgrade towards Olienhoutplaat
(21 January 1989)

Opposite: Garratt sunset: GMA/M (2 January 1988).
Above: Their work over for the day, a brace of 15F 4-8-2s drop their fires on the ashpit at Krugersdorp shed
before seeking refuge in the shed building for the night (12 January 1984)

Above: Twilight's liquid colours reflect in the waters of the Swartvlei, near Sedgefield.
Class 24 2-8-4s No. 3669 and No. 3652 (4 April 1986).
Opposite: 25NC No. 3479 forges through Mareetsane with a Vryburg–Mafikeng freight (22 November 1987)

Opposite: Two views of GMA/M No. 4072, near Zebra on a charter train destined for George (9 April 1985).
Above: The setting sun nestles between a pair of 25NCs
as they climb northwards at The Horn, near Witput (2 August 1985)

Above: 15F 4-8-2 No. 3077 nears Leslie on a Bethal–Springs freight
as the sun calls it a day (4 May 1985).
Opposite: Pure gold illuminates the sides of No. 3454 and No. 3511 as they pile it on through Petrusburg (23 July 1988)

It was touch and go whether No. 3511 and No. 3454
would reach the photographer at Driekloof before the last rays of the sun vanished
on 21 January 1989. They made it – just!

Tailpiece –
a rather unusual angle of 19D 4-8-2 No. 3338 at Cold Spring
on a Grahamstown–Alicedale mixed train (8 August 1985)

Index to Locomotive Classes

During Autumn 1990,
16DA 4-6-2 No. 879 is seen near Springs
on a freight from Bethal

Bibliography

The undermentioned books were consulted during the preparation of this work:

(Anonymous)
'Great South African
Steam Train Festival'
(South African Railways)

De Jong, R.C./van der Waal, G.M./
Heydenrych, D.H.
'NZASM 100'
(Chris van Rensburg Publications 1988)

(Internal Publication)
'Private Working Time Book No. 113:
Cape Northern Region'
(South African Transport Services)

Paxton, L./Bourne, D.
'Locomotives of
the South African Railways'
(C. Struik 1985)

Middleton, J.N.
'Industrial Steam Locomotives
of South Africa 1988'
(RSSA Preservation Group 1988)

Middleton, J.N.
'S.A.R. Locomotive Allocations 1989'
(RSSA Preservation Group 1989)

'S.A. Rail' Various issues

Various Contributors
'Off the beaten track'
(AA The Motorist Publications 1987)

Veterans Day! NZASM 14-tonner 'Emil Kessler' and ZASM 'B' No. 61
stand in steam at Germiston shed amongst the everyday shunting locomotives prior to working
the final train of the Z.A.S.M. centenary celebrations (Autumn 1990)

The Final Sunset

'Main line steam operations . . .

must inevitably come to an end . . .

The current steam working

between Kimberley and De Aar . . .

will be maintained until

. . . 1992'

*(Extracts from S.A.T.S. policy document
on steam traction issued during 1989)*

THE SEMAPHORE FALLS

THE COLOURS OF DAYLIGHT FADE

THE LAST SMOKE TRAIL RECEDES

. . . THE FINAL SUNSET OF STEAM

Witput, 1992??